Guide to Open Content Licenses

"There is a specter haunting cultural production, the specter of open content licensing"

Karl Marx (reworked for the digital era)

Lawrence Liang

guide to open content licenses

Piet Zwart Institute
institute for postgraduate studies and research
Willem de Kooning Academy Hogeschool Rotterdam

Table of Contents

Introduction 7

Chapter 1
The Black and White (and Grey) of Copyright 13

Chapter 2
Copyleft contextualised 23

Chapter 3
General Characteristics of Open Content Licenses 41

Chapter 4
Mapping Out the Domain of Open Content Licenses 53

Chapter 5
A Comparative Guide to Key Open Content Licenses 61

Further reading 97

Glossary 103

Introduction

In recent years ***copyright*** has moved away from being an esoteric and technical legal subject to one that affects musicians, designers, artists, students, authors, ordinary consumers, and more generally any one involved in any way in cultural production. Copyright stories assault us everyday in our newspapers, our emails and in the next few years, will play a very important role in determining the way we think of creativity; either in terms of property or in terms of collaboration. It is an issue in which content creators have a vital stake and certainly too important an issue to leave to the lawyers alone.
This booklet serves as an introduction to the world of '***open content*** licensing', a paradigm that is rapidly emerging as an important alternative to the existing model of copyright.

The world of open content licensing (which we shall consider in detail as we go along) has great benefits for a large number of people. You could for instance be:

- The creator of a website who wants it to be available indefinitely as a free, public resource. You would like to allow anyone to mirror your site or use its content for other projects without needing to obtain permission. After the creator's death mirroring or continuing the site should not be illegal for 70 years just because of standard copyright regulations.
- A musician or part of a band that wants to make your music available to a larger audience, and you decide that making it available online would be a good idea. But yet you may want to ensure that no one makes any

commercial use of your music without your permission.

- A part-time photographer or designer who has no problem with any person using your work or sharing it with others as long as they acknowledge your authorship and give you proper credit for it whenever they use your work.
- A documentary or experimental filmmaker willing to share your footage with others, and allowing them to use portions while making their films.
- Someone looking at using existing images, music, videos etc and mixing them with other content to create a remix or a new version, but who cannot afford to pay the high royalty or be someone interested in having people from other backgrounds use your work, or incorporate it into theirs.
- An artist whose work fundamentally depends on the ability to use existing material to create parodies, spoofs or subversions.
- A designer looking at collaborating with either another designer or just someone from a completely different discipline, by using or incorporating their work.
- A teacher interested in making your course syllabus available for others to use, so that they comment, add, critique it, or even work collaboratively with you to create an improvement on the course.
- A scholar, critic or essayist who wants his writing to be publicly accessible, to schools libraries and the general public instead of signing over copyrights to academic journal and book publishers who normally do not pay their authors, but make public institutions pay a lot of money for these publications.
- A playwright interested in writing an experimental play

through an online collaboration model and interested in ensuring that the play is available for everyone to use, but also concerned that any person who creates a version of your play should also allow others the same freedom of modifying or adapting this play that they have written.
- Or just someone in the world of cultural production who is sick of the dominant system of copyright and wants to explore other options.

But hey, what is wrong with the world of copyright anyway, and why should we even begin to start thinking in terms of alternatives to it? After all isn't copyright a system that exists primarily to protect creators and provide them with an incentive to produce?

While an initial purpose of copyright may have been to provide an incentive for creators, it is important not to be taken in completely by this mythical claim made by copyright. Consider for instance the following:

- Most creators/ authors are rarely the owners of their own copyright. It usually gets transferred to either the recording company, the publisher, or the person commissioning a work of art etc. Even in countries where copyright may, by law, be non-transferable, most publishers effectively circumvent this regulation by requiring the author to sign a contract which grants the publisher exclusive distribution rights.
- Musicians often make most of their money from live performances rather than from ***royalties*** from sales of their records. They sell 'services', as do many programmers and designers.

- And of course, monetary incentive is rarely the only reason for a person to be in cultural production. Besides, an open content model does not preclude you from making money off your work.

Copyright began as a system of balances to provide incentives to creators while also ensuring that there was a free circulation of works in the ***public domain***, which all other creators could build upon. For example, copyright explicitly allowed (and still allows) public libraries to exist as an alternative, non-commercial distribution channel for cultural works. Over time, this balance has shifted drastically in favour of content owners such as large publishing houses, media conglomerates etc. In fact copyright is often used as a tool to prevent or curb creativity and the move away from copyright is an important one in that it seeks to refocus on the interest of the general public as well as artists and creators.

Chapter 1

the black and white (and grey) of copyright

In a broad historical and cultural view, copyright is a recent and by no means universal concept. Copyright laws originated in Western society in the Eighteenth century. During the Renaissance, printers throughout Europe would reprint popular books without obtaining permissions or paying royalties and copyright was created as a way to regulate the printing industry. With the emergence of the concept of artistic genius, copyright became enmeshed with the general cultural understanding of authorship. Later, with globalized capitalism, control over copyrighted works became centered in the hands of media corporations instead of authors and artists. Even as the internet and digital media rendered distinctions between original and copies largely obsolete, changes in the law tried to artificially maintain them. As a result, copyright laws over time have been transformed from their original purpose of regulating the publishing industry to instead regulating its customers, artists and audiences.

Traditionally, copyright was of little relevance to cultural and artistic practice except in the realm of commercial print publishing. Some examples:

Authorship, originality and copyright are of no or little relevance in virtually all traditional forms of popular culture all over the world. Most folk songs and folktales, for example, are collective anonymous creations in the public domain. Variations, modifications and translations are traditionally encouraged as part of their tradition.

The Walt Disney Corporation founded much of its wealth on folk tales, such as *Snow White* and *Sinbad*, by taking them out of the public domain and turning them into ***proprietary***, copyrighted films and merchandise products. Today, the company is one of the strongest backers and political lobby sponsors for drastic copyright restrictions on digital media.

The same is true for many works considered part of the high-cultural canon, crafted by unidentified, often collective authors: Homer's epics for example, or the *Tales of 1001 Nights* which were spread by storytellers and of which no authoritative, 'original' written version ever existed. Modern philology believes them to be derived from Persian sources which in return were translated from Indian works.

In the Middle Ages and Renaissance, original authorship was even rather more disregarded than encouraged. In the foreword to *Don Quixote*, Cervantes falsely claims that his novel was based on an Arabic source. Literary works typically render themselves canonical by not inventing new stories, but rewriting existing ones, such as the many adaptions of *Faustus* from Christopher Marlowe to Johann Wolfgang Goethe, Fernando Pessoa, Alfred Jarry, Thomas Mann and Michel Butor.

Until the 20th century and the rise of the recording industry, copyright played no major role for music and musical composition. Musical themes were freely adapted and copied from one composer to another. Bach's *Concerto in D Major BWV 972* for example is simply a re-orchestration of the ninth movement of Vivaldi's *L'Estro Armonica*. Even as late as in the 19th century, Beethoven didn't have to buy a ***license*** for writing the *Diabelli Variations*, 83 variations on a waltz written by the Austrian Anton Diabelli. And finally the entire genre of Blues music is, as a matter of fact, a variation of only one song, the twelve bar harmonic scheme.

Copyright was a non-issue in the visual arts, too, until recently. Renaissance and baroque paintings were to a large degree collective workshop productions, and recycled conventionalized, emblematic pictorial motifs. Rubens and Rembrandt were the most prominent practitioners of the workshop method, with author ***attributions*** of their work remaining unclear until today. In 1921, Kurt Schwitters called his own brand of Dada 'Merz', derived from the logo of the German bank 'Commerzbank' which he had used in a collage painting. Today's artists who do the equivalent in the Internet risk being sued for copyright and trademark ***infringement***.

Ever since personal computers and the Internet closed most of the technical gaps that prevented media consumers from becoming media producers, and receiver technology from functioning as sender technology (to cite the media critiques of Bertolt Brecht and Hans Magnus Enzensberger from 1930's and 1970's), copyright has emerged as a deterrent against creativity rather than an incentive for it.

The case of the graphic artist Kieron Dwyer shows what might have happened to Kurt Schwitters if he had appropriated the bank logo nowadays. A year after Dwyer made comic books, t-shirts, and stickers with his version of the Starbucks logo, the company sued him. When the case was finally settled, Dwyer was allowed to continue displaying his logo, but only in extremely limited circumstances. No more comic books, t-shirts or stickers: he may post the image on the web, but not on his own website, nor may he link from his website to any other site that shows the parody. (Sources: **http://www.illegal-art.org**)

Alice Randall, a black American author wrote a parody of *Gone With the Wind* from the perspective of Scarlett O Hara's Mullato half sister. The estate of *Gone With the Wind* author Margaret Mitchell claimed that this was an infringement of copyright and obtained an injunction against →

the publication of the book. Fortunately in this case the court of appeal then overturned the injunction.

In December 2003, a young artist DJ Danger Mouse remixed an album called the *Grey Album* from the *White Album* of the Beatles and hip hop artist Jay Z's *Black Album*. Only 3000 copies of the *Grey Album* were released and would probably have disappeared into obscurity, were it not for the fact that two months later DJ Danger Mouse received a ***cease and desist letter*** ordering him to stop any further distribution of the album since it violated the copyright of the Beatles *White Album*, owned by EMI.

This unofficial ban on the album was seen as an unfair violation of creative expression by a number of people, and a campaign called *Grey Tuesday*, sponsored by **http://www.downhillbattle.org** was launched to ensure that the album would still be available for people to download via ***P2P*** networks. Over 170 web sites offered to host the *Grey Album*, many of which later received cease and desist letters from EMI. To date, the *Grey Album* has been downloaded by over 1.25 million users and continues in making DJ Danger Mouse the top 'selling' artists of the past year beating other contenders such as Norah Jones.

What then are our options in the face of this onslaught of copyright law? We could of course reject the legitimacy of these laws which impinge on freedom of speech and expression, but there is the danger of having to defend yourself in a highly expensive law suit.

This would still be a defensive move that relies on existing provision of copyright law, which makes our choices rather restricted. There is however another movement which is growing in popularity which recognizes the need for a pro-active approach towards building a public domain of materials which can be used in the future without necessarily having to obtain prior permission from the copyright owner or having to pay hefty royalties. It seeks to counteract the unrestricted growth of copyright. This movement is sometimes popularly called the ***copyleft*** movement. Its historical roots lie in free software (such as Linux and GNU), but more recently, it attempts to broaden its scope and apply the principles of free distribution, usage and collaborative development, to all kinds of media. In addition, there is also an artistic tradition of non- and anti-copyright:

The French late romantic poet Lautréamont wrote in a famous passage of his 1870 book *Poésies*: "*Plagiarism is necessary, progress implies it. It closely grasps an author's sentence, uses his expressions, deletes a false idea, replaces it with a right one*". Today, this reads like a precise description of how, for example, free software development works.

Inspired by Lautréamont and a study about gift economies by the French anthropologist Marcel Mauss, the Situationist International, a group of left-wing artists, cultural theorists and political activists that existed from 1958 to 1970, put all its publications under anti-copyright terms that permitted anyone to copy, translate and rewrite them even without authorization.

In the late 1980s and early 1990s, musicians and groups like Jon Oswald, Negativeland and the Tape-beatles advocated 'Plunderphonics', non-copyrighted music that mainly consisted of experimental audio collages of pop music and broadcasted sound material.

In 1999, the novel *Q* appeared under the name of Luther Blissett, known previously as the collective moniker of an Italian media prankster project. This allegorical account of Italian subculture in the form of a historical thriller set in 16th century Italy, *Q* became a national no.1 best-seller and subsequently appeared in French, German and English translations. Obviously, the sales didn't suffer at all from the fact that the imprint of the book permitted anyone to freely copy it for non-commercial purposes. What's more, the book was not released by an underground publisher, but by the well-established publishing houses Einaudi in Italy, Editions du Seul in France and Piper →

in Germany, amongst others who apparently didn't mind giving up traditional copyright-granted distribution models for a promising publication.

This introductory guide is meant for media designers, artists, musicians, producers of content, academics, researchers, etc. who are likewise interested in having their works widely circulated without too many restrictions. The model that it seeks to look at is the idea of the 'Open Content License'. But making your work available without placing restrictions does not however mean that you abandon your copyright to the work. This guide will provide a set of options to assert some rights to your work. It will also introduce the new positive rights to share, distribute and change being developing under copyleft.

Chapter 2

contextualising copyleft

So what exactly is copyleft or the open content model? While copyright has been in existence for nearly three hundred years, it is only in the past few years that it has become a subject of everyday discussion. These changes have primarily occurred as a result of the wide ranging changes brought on by the internet and by cheaper technologies of reproduction like CD writers. Disputes around file sharing, inaugurated by the Napster case for instance, have brought the discourse of copyright literally into the living rooms of ordinary people.

This movement of copyright from a techno-legal field into one that affects us on a day to day basis has foregrounded the politics of information and the control structure of copyright as well as alternatives to the copyright regime. If copyright originally emerged as a system of balance between providing sufficient incentive for ***authors*** and ***creators***, and the larger public interest of having free availability and flow of information in the public domain, a number of scholars feel that there has been a radical shift in this balance in favour of the owners of content, rather than that of the public.

It is important to remember that more often than not copyright is owned not by the authors themselves but by large corporations, the publishers, the record companies etc., and of course it is in the interests of the large players in the content industry to ensure that copyright extends its breadth and increases is depth. Two ways in which we have seen this increase is in the duration of copyright (from an initial fourteen years protection to effectively over ninety years now) as well as in its scope (copyright has extended to newer areas which it initially did not cover such as software, while at the same time controlling more rights than it was initially supposed to).

Free Software: Copyright Rearticulated

There is considerable scholarship done in documenting the expansion of copyright laws over the years, and for those interested there is a list of additional readings that you may refer to in the back of this book. The focus of this guide however takes off from the story of the extension of copyright, and the various responses that have emerged against the model of protection offered by copyright. The Free/Libre and Open Source (***FLOSS***) model in particular has emerged as a strong counter imagination to the dominant discourse of copyright, one that opens up alternative modes through which we can think of the question of knowledge production and distribution.

While phrases such as 'free software' and 'copyleft' conjure up an image of alternatives to copyright, it is relevant to note that it is not a model that abandons copyright. In fact quite the opposite, it relies on copyright law, but uses it creatively to articulate a positive, rather than a negative rights discourse. What do I mean by this?

Copyright has traditionally been an exclusive right that is granted to the owner of copyright to exploit his/ her work. Copyright is usually thought of as a bundle of rights that are available to the owner, and these are:

1. **Reproduction rights**: the right to reproduce copies of the work (for example making copies of a book from a manuscript)

2. **Adaptation rights**: the right to produce derivative works based on the copyrighted work (for example creating a film based on a book)
3. **Distribution rights**: the right to distribute copies of the work (for example circulating the book in bookshops)
4. **Performance rights**: the right to perform the copyrighted work publicly, (for example having a reading of the book or a dramatic performance of a play)
5. **Display rights**: the right to display the copyrighted work publicly (for example showing a film or work of art)

While copyright is available only to 'original works of authorship', for the purposes of copyright law, originality does not have the same meaning that it does in ordinary literal use as signifying a process of creativity. For copyright law, originality only refers to the fact that the work was not copied from another, or to the 'point of origin'. Thus as long as it can be shown that the work was not copied from another person's work, and that there is some labour involved in creating the work, then the requirement of originality has been satisfied.

Another important dimension is that there are no procedural requirements for obtaining copyright, it vests automatically with the creator the moment the work has been created and fixed in some tangible form. This can be a very serious problem. For instance I have made a useful graphic file and posted it on the internet. Even if I don't have a problem with any person downloading the file and using it for any purposes, such as including it in a teaching pack or on their homepage, the law of copyright is such that someone who uses the graphic without my permission, would be infringing my copyright. It may be that I choose not to prosecute them, but what has effectively happened is that the rule of exclusion has become the default rule in copyright. We have effectively moved away from a time when everything was presumed to be in the public domain unless otherwise stated, to a system where everything is presumed to be protected unless otherwise stated.

Licenses and the Control of Copyright

At this point it is useful for us to return to the story of the extension of copyright law. Given the fact that copyright as a bundle of rights includes so many rights, it basically becomes impossible for any person to use another's work without running into the danger of being an 'infringer'. Thus one needs to obtain a license from the owner of copyright to use any portion of the work. A license in copyright law is basically the grant of a right by the owner of copyright which allows the recipient of the license, the licensee, to exercise certain rights with respect to the copyrighted work. Without this license any use not granted by copyright by default would, be considered an infringement.

Derived from the Latin word 'licere', to allow, 'license' literally means 'permission'. Theoretically, a license can only permit things that copyright law places under the provision of the copyright owner and doesn't already permit by default. A license can thus only allow more, not less than the default copyright regulations. Free software and open content licenses therefore are licenses in the proper sense of the word. Proprietary software licenses however are even more restrictive than default copyright regulation. The Microsoft End User License Agreement (EULA) for instance allows you to install the software on one CPU alone, you cannot transfer it onto another computer and you certainly can not do anything which allows you to look at the ***source code*** of the computer program to understand the way it works etc.

```
Distribution. You may not distribute copies of
the SOFTWARE PRODUCT to third parties.

Prohibition on Reverse Engineering, Decom-
pilation, and Disassembly. You may not
reverse engineer, decompile, or disassemble
the SOFTWARE PRODUCT, except and only to
the extent that such activity is expressly
permitted by applicable law notwithstanding
this limitation.

Rental. You may not rent, lease, or lend the
SOFTWARE PRODUCT
```

End-user license agreement Microsoft Internet Explorer version 5.2, and software related components

How is it possible that such a 'license' is not a permission, but imposes additional restrictions? The catch lies in the term 'license agreement', which shifts the whole matter from copyright to contract law. By making you click on a box that you agree on the terms of the license agreement, software vendors make you sign a usage contract with them, thus circumventing even the scarce '***fair use***' liberties granted by copyright law (such as public lending of works in libraries).

Copyleft and open content licenses however do not really

circumvent copyright law, but, as stated before, work only within the legal framework of copyright legislation. What does this mean in practical terms? Even the best free software and open content license cannot protect you from legal claims of a third party against you, be it for copyright, contract, trademark or patent violation. In other words, if you create, like Kurt Schwitters, an art movement 'Merz' from the logo of the German Commerzbank, and put your Merz logo under an open content license, Commerzbank will still be able to sue you for trademark and possibly copyright violation. If you created a work for your employer and put it under an open license, or create a free variant of your original work, your employer might still sue you for contract violation if your work contract says that all your work belongs to him. If you create an open content website that has a one-click-online order function, Amazon.com can still sue you for infringement on its one-click patent. If you are a critic and need still photographs from a film you are writing about, making your work open content doesn't solve the problem that you need the reproductions rights for these images (unless they were put under an open content license themselves). Even if you get clearance for these rights, you will normally not be able to make your publication open content because that would violate the copyrights on the images.

All these severe problems can only be solved on a higher level, through a radical change of the international copyright framework in order to re-establish fundamental rights for fair and public use in the digital realm. Copylefting offers only a pragmatic solution within the existing framework, by creating a subcultural island of freely usable and distributable works within the larger sea of non-free media culture. Since any work which you don't copyleft is copyrighted by default and without your having to do anything, the limited solution might however still be better than not dealing with the issue at all.

The GNU GPL

It is within this highly rigid regime of copyright, that the Free Software movement sought to make an intervention. As a result, it has become highly popular across the world, and has become an inspiration for similar licensing models beyond the world of software. If the traditional software license specifically denies you certain rights, the GNU General Public License (GPL) is a license that that is designed to grant you certain fundamental freedoms. These are:

1. Users should be allowed to run the software for any purpose.
2. Users should be able to closely examine and study the software and should be able to freely modify and improve it to fill their needs better.
3. Users should be able to give copies of the software to other people to whom the software will be useful.
4. Users should be able to freely distribute their improvements to the broader public so that they, as a whole, benefit.

As you can see, the free software model differs drastically from the 'closed source' principles of licensing. Why then do we say that the GNU GPL model is based on an innovative use, rather than an abandonment of copyright? The Free Software model is predicated on ensuring that the fundamental freedoms are not taken away or removed from the public domain by anyone: and so they have a condition attached to the use of Free Software.

```
1. You may copy and distribute verbatim copies
of the Program's source code as you receive
it, in any medium, provided that you conspicu-
ously and appropriately publish on each copy
an appropriate copyright notice and disclaimer
of warranty; keep intact all the notices that
refer to this License and to the absence of any
warranty; and give any other recipients of the
Program a copy of this License along with the
Program.
(...)

2. You may modify your copy or copies of the
Program or any portion of it, thus forming
a work based on the Program, and copy and
distribute such modifications or work under the
terms of Section 1 above.
You may modify your copy or copies of the
Program or any portion of it, thus forming
a work based on the Program, and copy and
distribute such modifications or work under the
terms of Section 1 above
```

GNU General Public License
version 2, June 1991

The fundamental condition is that any person who uses free software to create a ***derivative work***, or an adaptation of the software must ensure that this software is also licensed on the same terms and conditions, namely under the GNU GPL. If the author of a piece of free software decided to relinquish his copyright, it would mean that someone could use his or her code and create a derivative work and then license it as a proprietary piece of code, therefore preventing others from making use of the software in a free manner.

Lastly, the word 'free' can sometimes be confusing as it often refers to pricing, but the word free as used in free software refers not to pricing but to freedom. Thus you can charge for free software (for instance the version of Linux distributed by Red Hat) or you can have software which is available free of cost but does not grant you any freedoms (Internet Explorer).

Challenges to copyright

What the free software movement did was use copyright in an innovative manner to ensure access, rather than restrict people's ability to use, distribute and modify code. At the heart of the free software movement lies a radical reworking of the very idea of the user. If in the realm of proprietary software the user was a passive consumer, the free software model is predicated on the idea of a user producer, a user who has the ability to contribute to the existing work and simultaneously become a producer as well. Copying, cutting and pasting, changing things, applying filters, and so on are part of the basic language of digital media. The user-producer is a concept that speaks to the digital experience and the freedoms that this digital culture allows for ordinary people to become artists and producers. This model fundamentally challenges the traditional assumptions of copyright law, it moves away from the idea of the romantic notion of authorship, which saw authorship and cultural production as an isolated activity of a genius sitting and creating something out of nothing. Instead it argues that the very essence of cultural production has been about learning from copying and producing by creatively using works that exist in the public domain. It also moves away from the mythical notion of the originality of the work to recognize the value that various users contribute through their modifications and adaptations to an existing work, thus placing a higher premium on collaborative production than on isolated production.

It is not as though the idea of collaborative production is a new one. In fact the history of cultural production has, to a large extent, been the history of collaborative production, and this is true in all kinds of human achievements. Take for instance a few simple illustrations:

- The *Oxford English Dictionary* (OED) was only possible through the collaborative efforts of hundreds of people from across the world. It did not bear the tag of being an open model of production, because it was created in a time when the myth of copyright backed by the power of large content owners had not engulfed the imagination of production.
- Often the grant of individual authorship renders invisible the role that a large number of people may have played in the creation of a work. For instance in the case of a film, a director is generally considered to be the author of a work but in reality a film is the product of the creative labour of a large number of people and in fact would be impossible without collaborative effort
- Hip hop has been about the ability to build on previous work by sampling and creating new works
- The world of dance is marked by a constant culture of borrowing and building on previous efforts
- Media design is constantly building upon and linking to the work of others

What was unique about the FLOSS model was that it used the copyright regime for the first time to express this aspect of collaborative production, and also afford it protection to ensure that it remained within the public domain. Having got rid of the heavy burden of the myth of copyright the challenge was then to translate the terms of the FLOSS model into other domains of cultural production. Translating the terms of the GNU GPL into other models of creative licensing which would enable people to act as collaborator/ producers rather than merely as passive users, and also ensure that there is a rich public domain of materials that people can use and build on for the future is what this pamphlet is about.

The Public Domain

We have been using the idea of the public domain. What exactly do we mean by that? For the purposes of understanding cultural production, the public domain could be understood as the body of works that we have access to, to create newer works. Thus while Shakespeare was a brilliant playwright we should also remember the fact that he drew rather liberally from various sources, from history, mythology and the works of his peers etc. as inspiration, and as sources to modify. Similarly even Walt Disney had a rich variety of courses that he could draw from to make his cartoon versions of *Fantasia*, *Steamboat Willie*, *Snow White and the Seven Dwarfs* etc. This public domain has also often been referred to through the metaphor of the '***Commons***', resources that are not divided into individual bits of property but rather are jointly held so that anyone may use them without special permission. Think of public streets, parks, waterways, outer space, and creative works in the public domain – all of these things are, in a way, part of the commons.

Open/ Collaborative Production

It is as a response to the shrinking of the public domain, through stronger enforcement of copyright laws, that the open source movement and the open content movement has emerged. What are some of the benefits of an open content model, and why would people want to license their works on an open content model, rather than relying on the traditional copyright model? There may be a number of reasons and advantages for wanting to do so.

- For most artists, authors, musicians or designers who are not already established, the easiest way to make a name for yourself is by ensuring that your work is seen by a large number of people, and by a wide range of audiences, as this helps to popularize your work, and establish your reputation. Open content licenses enables your work to circulate in a much wider manner than if there were restrictions on the work. Apart from making you more visible, this model of distribution also enables you to either obtain more shows, more work, sponsorship etc.

- Since the model of distribution relies, more often than not on a ***peer to peer*** system of sharing, it cuts out significant costs in terms of a middleman, an agent or a gallery who act as distributors. This is a system in which people can often contact the content creator directly rather than having to go through an institution or an individual who mediates on behalf of the content creator. Often creators who are struggling to establish themselves have no bargaining power with publishers, record companies, etc. since they do not have the ability to distribute on their own. The open content model combined with the powers of the internet are a great way for someone to establish themselves without having to rely on the big business model of authors and artists.

- More often than not, people do not create content only for monetary reasons. They do it to express themselves, to share their works, to get an idea across etc. In such cases, by licensing the work through an open content license, you have the ability to reach out to a much larger group of people as people can freely use your work, and distribute your work without the fear of violating your copyright. In an era where copyright litigation costs an average of $250,000[1] you can well imagine that people would feel more comfortable using freely available open content.

- But leaving aside the romance of altruism, assuming that you do want to make money out of your work, it is important to remember that free/ open content is not inconsistent with the ability for you to charge for your work. The licensing model allows enough flexibility for you to determine the manner in which you will license the use of your work. For instance while you may allow for academic uses and other not-for-profit use, (or even charge for them) you could reserve the right for any commercial usage, so that any person wanting to make commercial use of your work (for example bring out copies of a book, or use a design on a t-shirt or website, Thus you will still be able to charge for such usage.

- There are also cases of relatively unknown part time musicians such as Allan Vilhan from Slovakia, working under the name *Cargo Cult* who made their music available online for free, and receive donations from people who have enjoyed the music (this and many similar stories are available at the Creative Commons website **http://creativecommons.org**). Similarly Free Software developer Jaromil made photos that he had taken in Palestine available for free online, and has been approached by people who want to use them and were willing to pay for the usage. The internet model of distribution may seem like a disaster for large content companies or already established artists (even that is contestable) but for emerging artists or creators who do not have access to a great deal of capital investment, the internet is truly a godsend in terms of its ability to reach out to a large number of people at a relatively low cost.

- There have been some recent examples of how people make their works available for free online, and yet this has not affected their offline sales. Science fiction author Cory Doctorow took advantage of this trend when he released an online version of his book, *Down and Out in the Magic Kingdom* simultaneously with a print version of the book. The print version has done very well, and in fact it could even be argued that the print version has sold better as a result of the book having been distributed for free. It is very similar to allowing people to browse through a book in a shop before they decide whether they want to buy it. The lead was recently followed by Lawrence Lessig, the high priest of open cultures, who released a free online version of his book *Free Culture* along with the print copy. Within a few weeks, there were various adaptations of the work, in the form of posters, audio books etc which were also available for downloading.

- More and more people are realizing the value of collaborative content creation. By making their works available not only to a larger community of users but also a larger community of creators, they also realize that there is a value that is added to their work. Most open content licenses demand a detailed recording of the process of authorship, and every use of your work is also at the same time a record of your authorship. There is therefore a very significant attempt to move away from the binaries of originals and copies, to the idea of a rescension, a version or a re-mix which is neither a copy nor an original but instead a work that builds on existing work and yet has an autonomy of its own.

- Some people may want to use the open licenses model for distributing their content, simply because they are tired of the monopoly of the content industry and the limitations of the system of copyright. Thus the idea of being able to contribute to an intellectual commons may seem highly attractive. Some people may be attracted by the notion of others building upon their work, or by the prospect of contributing to an intellectual commons. This idealism has not inflicted just young people who are used to an age of access, but even established stars like George Michael, who recently announced that he was not going to produce any commercial music in the future and that all of his music in the future will be available for free via the internet.

- Very often we forget that a lot of content owners especially those in the world of academia or artists who benefit from endorsements grants from public bodies, are actually producing intellectual property using public resources. In such a case it is important for us to start thinking in terms of 'public intellectual property for public money'.

I will leave it to you to add to the reasons for choosing an open content model. But having chosen an open content model, the next question that obviously arises is what kind of a license should I use for my work. Thankfully the situation is not as difficult as in the free software world, where there exists a plethora of licenses to choose from. The open content model is still a relatively new development, and it has also had the fortune of having to learn from the experience of the free software model, and so the range of licenses are relatively manageable. Having said that for a layperson it can still be a little difficult to navigate through these various licenses.

This brief guide has been created to help you navigate through the world of open content licenses. Whilst the final decision will have to be yours, we hope that this little map helps in understanding the options and advantages of such a way of working.

[1] On the Average cost of defending an IP suit- in the US and in other countries: There are conflicting statistics on the same, and there are a number of places where the numbers differ. For instance Dan Ravisher of the Public Patent Foundation is cited as stating that such a case costs one million dollars. (From, Robin Arnfield, *Linux Patent-Infringement Threat Surfaces*, CIO Today, August 2nd 2004, **www.cio-today.com/story.xhtml?story_id=26129**). In *Free Culture*, (pg 51) Lawrence Lessig states that copyright cases routinely cost $250,000.

Chapter 3

general characteristics of open content licenses

Most open content licenses share a few common features that distinguish them from traditional copyright licenses. These can be understood in the following ways:

a. Basis of the license/ validity of the license.
b. Rights granted.
c. Derivative Works.
d. Commercial/ Non Commercial Usage.
e. Procedural Requirements imposed.
f. Appropriate Credits.
g. Open content licenses do not affect fair use rights.
h. Absence of ***warranty***.
i. Standard legal clauses.

a. Basis of the license/ validity of the license

While being a form of license that allows end users freedom, it is important to remember that the open content licenses, like free software licenses, are based on the author of a work having valid copyright. It is on the basis of this copyright and the exclusive rights that it grants him/her that the author can structure a license that allows him to impose the kinds of rights and obligations involved in using the work. Every open content license therefore asserts the copyright of the author and states that without a license from the author, any user using the work would be violation of copyright. Put negatively, such licenses cannot be used to violate copyright. Thus the usage of the work is subject to all the terms and conditions imposed by the license. Using this right, the open content licenses can then impose restrictions that ensure that the work is not used to create a derivative work which has restrictive conditions imposed on it. Most open content licenses also assert that an acceptance of the terms and conditions of the license need not be explicit, and may arise from the conduct of a user. Thus, in the case of a song, the moment you download the song you are bound by the terms of the open content license. The user cannot at a later date claim that s/he did not agree to the terms of the license.

b. Rights Granted

The premise of an open content license is that unlike most copyright licenses which imposes stringent conditions on the usage of the work, the open content licenses enable users to have certain freedoms by granting them rights. Some of these rights are usually common to all open content licenses such as the right to copy the work and the right to distribute the work. Depending on the particular license, the user may also have the right to modify the work, create derivative works, perform the work, display the work and distribute the derivative works. When choosing a license, the first thing that you will have to decide is the extent to which you are willing to grant someone rights over your work. For instance you have created a font, and do not have a problem if people create versions of it, then you can choose a license that grants the user all rights, but on the other hand if you are willing to allow people to copy the font and distribute it but you do not want them to change the typeface or create versions of it, then you will choose a more restrictive license which only grants them the first two rights.

c. Derivative Works

Any work that is based on an original work created by you is a derivative work. The key difference between different kinds of open content licenses is the method that they adopt to deal with the question of derivative works. This issue is an inheritance from the licensing issues in the free software movement. The GNU GPL for instance makes it mandatory that any derivative work created from a work licensed under the GNU GPL must also be licensed under the GNU GPL. This is a means of ensuring that no one can take the benefit of a 'free work' and then create a work, which can be licensed with restrictive terms and conditions. In other words, it ensures that a work that has been made available in the public domain cannot be taken outside of the public domain. On the other hand you may have a license like the BSD software license that may allow a person who creates a derivate work to license that derivative work under a proprietary or closed source license.

This ability to control a derivative work through a license is perhaps the most important aspect of the open content licenses. They ensure in a sense, a self perpetuity. Since a person cannot make a derivative work without your permission, your permission is granted on the condition that s/he also allows others to use the derivative work freely.

In open content licenses, the right to create a derivative work normally includes the right to create it in all media. Thus if I license a story under an open content license, I also grant the user the right to create an audio rendition of it.

The obligation to ensure that the derivative work is also licensed under the terms and conditions of the open content license are however not applicable in cases where the work is merely aggregated into a collection/ anthology/ compilation. For instance I have drawn and written comic called X, which is being included in a general anthology. In such a case the other comics in the anthology may be licensed under different terms, and the open content license is not applicable to them and will only be applicable to my comic X in the anthology.

d. Commercial/ Non Commercial Usage

Another important aspect of open content licenses is the question of commercial/ non commercial usages. I may for instance license a piece of video that I have made but only as long as the person is using it for non-commercial purposes. On the other hand a very liberal license may grant the person all rights, including the right to commercially exploit the work.

e. Procedural Requirements imposed

Most open content licenses require a very strict adherence to procedures that have to be followed by the end user if s/he wants to distribute the work, and this holds true even of derivative works. The licenses normally demand that a copy of the license accompanies the work, or the inclusion of some sign or symbol which indicates the nature of the license that the work is bring distributed under, for instance ◎, and information about where this license may be obtained. This procedure is critical to ensure that all the rights granted and all the obligations imposed under the license are also passed onto third parties who acquire the work.

f. Appropriate Credits

The next procedural requirement that has to be strictly followed is that there should be appropriate credits given to the author of the work. This procedure applies in two scenarios, the first is when the end user distributes the work to a third party, then s/he should ensure that the original author is duly acknowledged and credited. It also applies when the end user wants to modify the work or create a derivative work. Then the derivative work should clearly mention the author of the original and also mention where the original can be found.

The importance of this clause arises from the fact that while open content licenses seek to create an alternative ethos of sharing and collaboration, it also understands the importance of crediting the author. Very often in the absence of monetary incentive, other motivating factors such as recognition, reputation and honour become very important. Open content licenses, far from ignoring the rights of the author, insist on strict procedures so that these authorial rights are respected.

> You may copy and distribute the Document in any medium, either commercially or non-commercially, provided that this License, the copyright notices, and the license notice saying this License applies to the Document are reproduced in all copies, and that you add no other conditions whatsoever to those of this License. You may not use technical measures to obstruct or control the reading or further copying of the copies you make or distribute.

GNU Free Documentation License
version 1.2, November 2002

```
You may copy and distribute copies of the
Music as you receive it, in any medium,
provided that you:
(a) conspicuously and appropriately publish
on each copy an appropriate copyright notice;
(b) keep intact all the notices that refer to
this License;
(c) supply, with each copy of the Music,
all significant information about the Music,
including the title of the work, the name of
the artist, and the names and roles of all
credited personnel;
(d) supply, to each recipient of the Music,
along with the Music, either a copy of this
License or a clearly visible URL that lets
the recipient know where to find a copy of this
License on the Internet.
If the information required by (a) to (d)
above is not available, for example when the
Music has been received by making a recording
of a performance, then this information must
be obtained independently and no copies can
be made or distributed without this informa-
tion being included with each copy of the
Music.
```

Ethymonics Free Music License
version 1, August 2000

g. Open Content Licenses do not affect fair use rights

Under copyright law, there is an exception to infringement and this is known as the fair use exception. Fair use exceptions generally include using portions for critique or review, and certain non-commercial or educational academic uses etc. Open content licenses make it clear that the terms and conditions of the license do not affect your fair use rights. Thus even if someone is in disagreement with the terms and conditions, and refuses to enter into the open content license, s/he may still have the freedom to use the work to the extent that is allowed by the principles of his/her fair use rights.

```
The OpenMusic works may be reproduced and
distributed in whole or in part, in any medium
physical or electronic, provided that the
terms of this license are adhered to, and
that this license or an incorporation of it
by reference (with any options elected by the
author(s) and/or publisher) is displayed in
the reproduction.
```

LinuxTag Green OpenMusic License
draft v1.1, 22 April 2001

h. Absence of warranty

Since more often than not the work is being made available at no financial cost and also gives the user certain freedoms, most open content licenses have a standard clause which states that the work is being provided without any warranty or on a 'as is basis'. The licensor cannot be in a position to provide any warranty on the work. A few licenses however provide the end user the option of providing a warranty of services, or a warranty on the derivative work so long as that warranty is one between the licensee and the third party.

```
Because the opencontent (oc) is licensed
free of charge, there is no warranty for the
oc, to the extent permitted by applicable
law. Except when otherwise stated in writing
the copyright holders and/or other parties
provide the oc “as is” without warranty of any
kind, either expressed or implied, including,
but not limited to, the implied warranties of
merchantability and fitness for a particular
purpose. The entire risk of use of the oc is
with you. Should the oc prove faulty, inac-
curate, or otherwise unacceptable you assume
the cost of all necessary repair or correc-
tion.
```

OpenContent License (OPL)
version 1.0, July 14, 1998

```
The work is provided “as is,” and comes with
absolutely no warranty, express or implied,
to the extent permitted by applicable law,
including but not limited to the implied
warranties of merchantability or fitness for a
particular purpose.
```

Design Science License
1999-2001

i. Standard legal clauses

A few other clauses that appear at the end of most open content licenses are the standard legal clauses that are included in most legal agreements, and you don’t have to worry too much about them while choosing a license. These generally include :

- **Severability**: This means that even if one portion of the license is held to be invalid the other portions will still continue to have effect.
- Limitation on ***liability***: The licenses normally state that the licensor will not be liable for anything arising from the use of the work. Thus, for instance, an end user cannot claim that he suffered mental trauma as a result of the work.
- The licenses do not allow you to modify any portion of the license while redistributing works etc.
- **Termination**: Most licenses state that the rights granted to the licensee are automatically terminated the moment s/he violates any obligation under the license.

Chapter 4

mapping out the domain of open content licenses

There are various ways in which we can map out the various kinds of open content licenses. These are:

a. On the basis of the medium they address
b. On the nature of the license
c. On the validity of the license

As with any other attempt at mapping, the task can only be an imprecise one. Whilst we are making a broad map available for the user to help him/ her navigate through the licenses, we would also encourage you to read these licenses in their full text form. This will overcome the initial fear that legal language always instills in people. Instead it will allow you to see the license more as a possible narrative or as a piece of design in itself.

a. On the basis of the medium they address

The next manner in which we can group the open content licenses is by looking at the medium that the licenses seek to address. At the outset it must be stated that while choosing a license, you will first want to see whether it is a general license or a specific license. A general license can be seen as a 'One size fits all' kind of license where the specific nature of the content does not matter. You will be choosing the license not because it is specifically designed for the medium in which your work resides, say music, but for the content of the license. The open content, Creative Commons licenses are examples of general content licenses. The specific license on the other hand, is a license that is designed with a particular medium in mind. There are not a whole range of licenses in this segment, and most of the specialized licenses attempt to deal with the question of music. Thus within music, you have a choice of the EFF Free Audio License, the Ethymonics Free Music License, the Open Music licenses as well as the Creative Commons music license. It always make sense to choose a specific license over a general license as it may be more suited to your needs and addresses some of the nuanced requirements that may arise from a particular media.

b. On the nature of the license

Finally, the open content licenses can also be categorized according to the nature of the license. There are some licenses which may be closer to the principle of the GNU GPL, which means that they believe in 'absolute' freedom where there are very few restrictions that may be imposed on the work as well as the derivative work. Similarly there may be other licenses that grant the basic freedoms but then allow the licensor to impose restrictions on specialized rights such as commercial usage, creation of derivative works. Of course these divisions are never absolute, even within a class or family of licenses. Thus within the Creative Commons licenses for instance you may have a completely open license that allows for all rights, while you could also have license that allows certain rights, but imposes many restrictions as well.

c. On the validity of the license

One of the questions that has plagued the GNU GPL is the question of its validity. While this question is still to be answered in a court of law, it has become an important consideration that people bear in mind while drafting an open content license. An interesting development that we see in the world of open content licenses is that if one were to classify them chronologically as first generation (i.e. free art, open content, Open Audio) and second generation licenses (Creative Commons), within the shorter year spans of internet time, a significant shift in the style of second generation licenses can be seen.

> Knowledge and creativity are resources which, to be true to themselves, must remain free, i.e. remain a fundamental search which is not directly related to a concrete application. Creating means discovering the unknown, means inventing a reality without any heed to realism. Thus, the object(ive) of art is not equivalent to the finished and defined art object. This is the basic aim of this Free Art License: to promote and protect artistic practice freed from the rules of the market economy.

Free Art License
Preamble version 1.2

In many ways the first generation license were marked by a certain performative, polemical stance. What do I mean by this? When you read some of the earlier open content licenses they normally open with a crisp polemical statement, which acts both as the ***preamble*** to the license, as well as an ideological statement against copyright. They do not have the same impersonal feel that most documents written in legal language convey. In other words the license was like a speech act, where it was both the site of, as well as the reason for, a transformation in the way that we conceive production and distribution of knowledge. Most of the first generation licenses are however also probably less effective as legal documents than the second-generation licenses. But that is also what makes them interesting; they retain a certain edginess as licenses that seems to be absent in the more legally efficient second generation licenses.

> The licenses for most software are designed to take away your freedom to share and change it. By contrast, the GNU General Public License is intended to guarantee your freedom to share and change free software - to make sure the software is free for all its users.

GNU General Public License
preamble version 2, June 1991

The second generation licenses have been rendered 'professional'. They look, sound and feel more like a legal document. And given the fact that the licenses are supposed to be the primary building blocks for shared creation, this is a very important factor as well, that the licenses should stand good in a court of law. It is as though the license has been cleansed of its performative value, and the ideological battle happens outside the narrative structure of the license.

```
The work (as defined below) is provided under
the terms of this creative commons public
license ("ccpl" or "license"). The work is
protected by copyright and/or other appli-
cable law. Any use of the work other than as
authorized under this license or copyright
law is prohibited. By exercising any rights
to the work provided here, you accept and
agree to be bound by the terms of this
license. the licensor grants you the rights
contained here in consideration of your
acceptance of such terms and conditions.
```

Creative Commons License
preamble version 2.0

The idea is not to make a trivial point about language or rhetorical statements in the license, the larger point is to look at these developments or movements towards a more formal mode in the second generation licenses as also mapping out the larger debate on copyright. For some of us the battle over copyright is not merely about the future of creativity, but ties into the larger future of capital as it seeks to create new ways to extend property, and this process of 'cleaning up the licenses' also often means an inability to deal with practices which reside on the murkier parts of the legal arena. What we need to avoid is a situation where open content licenses almost result in a gentrification of the debate on copyright.

Chapter 5

a comparative guide to key open content licenses

The licenses are classified in the following manner:
The first section deals with the 'first generation' licenses while the second section deals introduces the 'second generation' licenses (See Chapter 3, section c.). A number of the initial licenses have now been incorporated within the Creative Commons licenses, and these are included in the appendix. While they are not in use anymore, they are interesting to study for reason of understanding the transition from the first to the second generation license.

Please note that every license listed in the next chapter also includes a description of the procedure to be followed if you are to use that license (usually found at the end of the license).

Free Art License

Version 1.1

http://artlibre.org/license.php/lalgb.html

Perhaps one of the first initiatives at translating some of the Free/ Open Source ideas outside of the domain of software and into the domain of art, this license, describes itself as the license with a Copyleft attitude.

The Free Art license was born out of the meeting *Copyleft Attitude* in Paris in 2000. These meetings brought together for the first time, computer specialists and free software activists along with contemporary artists and members of the art world. The license allows artist/ creators to make their works available freely to the public, and grants them the right to copy, distribute and modify the work if certain conditions are met.

Philosophy of the Free Art License

The preamble states that "`Whereas current literary and artistic property rights result in restriction of the public's access to works of art, the goal of the Free Art License is to encourage such access`". The license is also designed to enable the public to make creative use of art works, therefore reinforcing the idea of the user/ producer model of the internet and other digital media. It also recognizes that with the birth of the internet, there are greater possibilities of collaboration, shared and distributed production etc., traditional copyright does not facilitate such collaborations. The Free Art License "`Also encourages a continuation of the process of experimentation undertaken by many contemporary artists`".

The Free Art License advocates an economy appropriate for art, based on sharing, exchange and joyful giving. It says "`What counts in art is also and mostly what is not counted`".

Rights Granted

An artist/ creator using the Free Art License grants the user the following freedoms:

1. Freedom to make copies of the work for personal use or the use of others
2. Freedom to distribute the work on any medium. This right is applicable both to modified and unmodified works. The person distributing may do it either for free or charge for the distribution.
3. Freedom to modify the work as long as the same preconditions as mentioned above are met.

The freedom to distribute and the right to modify are however subject to the following conditions:
The licensee has to attach the license in its entirety or indicate where it can be found

- Specify the name of the author of the original
- Specify to the recipient where he can access the originals

How does it work

The license envisages enabling a continuation of the process of the creation of art. This is counter-posed to an idea of art as simply an end result oriented activity. Therefore it establishes the following model:

Original Work → **Subsequent works** (based on original) → **Communal work**

To ensure that any work that is used under the Free Art License does not get taken out of the public domain, the license prohibits the incorporation of the license into any art work which is not licensed under the same terms and conditions as the Free Art License. Thus a person who creates a subsequent work based on an original work cannot then attempt to remove it from the public domain. That work has to be licensed under the Free Art License.

The Free Art License imposes this restriction not to deny any person his contribution or authorial rights but by choosing to contribute to the evolution of this work of art, the licensee/ user agrees to give to others the same rights which were also granted to the licensee.

The Free Art License clearly states that no person has any right to use any of the works without accepting the terms and conditions of the license. The moment they accept then they are bound to follow the terms of the license. Acceptance does not have to be explicitly stated, it can also be by the way of an act such as copying, distributing or modifying the work.

Why use the Free Art license?
The Free Art License offers a useful legal protocol to prevent abusive appropriation. It will no longer be possible for someone to appropriate your work, short-circuiting the creative process to make personal profit from it. Helping yourself to a collective work in progress will be forbidden, as will monopolising the resources of an evolving creation for the benefit of a few. Expressed positively, this is a good license to use to contribute to a cultural public domain.

Documentation Licenses

While not cultural production in the classical sense, it is important to briefly speak about and understand free documentation licenses. As anyone who has tried learning to use software will know, an important aspect of the software also lies in the documentation that is available for it. These licenses, whilst not being medium-specific, are targeted at this form of publication, but may possibly be useful for documenting things other than software.

GNU Free Documentation License

Version 1.2, November 2002
http://www.gnu.org/copyleft/fdl.html

The GNU Free Documentation License serves primarily as a supplement or a complementary license to the GNU GPL. It is intended primarily for manuals or other instructional texts or documents which have a 'functional value'. Given its subject matter, the license is also a little technically confusing for the lay reader. It would be better to avoid this license if your work is more in the nature of a literary work. One of the Creative Commons licenses would be more appropriate to use for such works.

Philosophy
Since free software needs free documentation: a free program should come with manuals providing the same freedoms that the software does. This license seeks to make manuals, instructional texts or other functional and useful documents 'free' in the sense of freedom.

Rights granted
There are three principle goals of the license:

1. Grants everyone the effective freedom to copy and redistribute it, commercially or non-commercially with or without modifying it
2. The License preserves for the author and publisher a way to get credit for their work, while not being con sidered responsible for modifications made by others
3. This License is a 'copyleft' license, which means that derivative works of the document must themselves be free in the same sense.

How does it work?
However the GNU Free Documentation license is a very cumbersome one in terms of the procedural requirements that it places on a user, as well as being a difficult license to read for a lay person. It still serves as the best license for software documentation, but for any other kinds of instructional literature, like a textbook, I would recommend using a Creative Commons license rather than the GNU Free Documentation license. A number of the provisions in this license are designed specifically with software manuals in mind and may not have significance for other instructional manuals. This is specially true with respect to the requirements that it has on the different segments of a work and procedures to be followed for the same.

All in all the GNU Free Documentation License is useful as a complementary license to be used with software that has been licensed under the terms of the GNU GPL. For users with such requirements it is useful to consult the license directly.

Common Documentation License

Version 1.0, February 16, 2001

http://www.opensource.apple.com/cdl

A documentation license brought out by Apple for software documentation, instructional manuals etc. It seeks to be a much neater and simpler license than the GNU Free Documentation License by avoiding a number of the elaborate technical details of publishing which are required there.

Philosophy

A straight forward documentation license. It says that "`To preserve simplicity, the License does not specify in detail how (e.g. font size) or where (e.g. title page, etc.) the author should be credited`"

What does it apply to

Any documentation, manual or other work that contains a notice placed by the Copyright Holder stating that it is subject to the terms of this Common Documentation License

Rights Granted

The license grants the following rights:

The right to copy, modify, publicly display, distribute and publish the Document and the Derivative Works in any medium physical or electronic, commercially or non-commercially; provided that:

- all copyright notices in the Document are preserved;
- a copy of this License, or an incorporation of it by reference in proper form is included in a conspicuous location in all copies such that it would be reasonably

viewed by the recipient of the Document; and
- You add no other terms or conditions to those of this License.

How does it work?

All derivative works have to be released under the terms and conditions of this license, and all appropriate notices regarding the license and the changes are retained.

The work and the derivative work may be compiled in a compilation. If it is a mere aggregation, then the other works in the compilation shall not be subject to the terms and conditions of this license. However all notices regarding the applicability of this license to the work/ derivative work shall be retained.

EFF Open Audio License

Version 1.0.1, text version.
There is no substantive change from ver. 1.0[.0] and only typographic errors have been corrected.
http://www.eff.org/IP/Open_licenses/eff_oal.php

The EFF Open Audio license is a license that is based on the GNU GPL for music and other audio works.

The EFF (Electronic Freedom Foundation) is a non profit activist group involved in campaigning, litigating and advocating on various electronic rights, ranging from online privacy, fighting against digital rights management (a technology directed at 'protecting copyright'), as well as advocating alternative models of production and distribution.

Philosophy of the Open Audio License

The preamble states the general principles of copyleft very clearly, and also argues for why there is a need for innovative licensing mechanisms that allows people to share their works in the context of the digital revolution. It is intended to help create a vibrant public domain in which there will be easy availability of works which people can build upon. The license sees it self as:

> "A tool of freedom for artists who wish to reach one another and new fans with their original works. It allows musicians to collaborate in creating a pool of 'open audio' that can be freely modified, exchanged, and utilized in new ways. Artists can use this license to promote themselves and take advantage of the new possibilities for empowerment and independence that technology provides.

> It also allows the public to experience new music, and connect directly with artists, as well as enable 'super distribution' where the public is encouraged to copy and distribute a work, adding value to the artist's reputation while experiencing a world of new music never before available".

The preamble also makes it clear that while EFF is uncomfortable with licensing as opposed to sale, this license differs from the usual copyright licenses in that it is designed specifically to achieve the goals of making more works accessible and available for use and modification.

How does it work?

The license is applicable for any work that is released under the EFF Open Audio license, and marked as ◎. When used for a sound recording, the license covers both the copyright in both the sound recording (the 'master' rights) and the underlying musical composition (the 'songwriter' rights).

Rights Granted

The license grants the following rights:

1. Right to access/ use the work
2. Right to copy or reproduce the work
3. Right to distribute the work
4. Right to modify the work or create derivative works
5. Right to publicly perform the work in any medium (This also extends to derivative works)

Provided:

- The identity of the original author should be acknowledged and all details retained.

This can be done either through a physical medium such as on the album cover or by embedding the details in the digital file.

- That any new work created which is either derived from or contains, any part of the original work, then it must be licensed under the same terms and conditions as this license. This does not apply in the case of a mere aggregation (as in the case of an anthology for instance).

Open Music Licenses

http://openmusic.linuxtag.org/showitem.php?item=209

The Open Music license is an initiative from Germany that attempts to replicate the GNU GPL into the domain of music but provides for a set of customized licenses (represented in as Green, Yellow, Red and Rainbow) depending on the nature of rights that are allowed by the license.

Philosophy

To enable musicians to share their works and allow people to use the music, but also ensuring that musicians retain enough control to make money from their music.

The OpenMusic License was drafted after consultations with several songwriters, musicians and bands. While the core of the license remains the ability to allow people to use and distribute OpenMusic, the licenses then break up into three primary colours, which follow the logic of traffic signal lights.

- The **Green License** gives the go ahead for almost any kind of use
- The **Yellow License** allows all rights but prevents commercial exploitation
- The **Red License** only allows for personal use and distribution

There is a fourth option which is a do it yourself, mix and match license called the **Rainbow License**. Once you are familiar with the basic three colours, then you can create your own rainbow licenses.

Rights granted	**Green**	**Yellow**	**Red**
Private use	•	•	•
Private Modification	•	•	
Private derived Works	•	•	
Private Distribution	•	•	•
Private Broadcasting	•	•	•
Commercial Use	•		
Commercial Modification	•		
Commercial derived works	•		
Commercial Distribution	•		
Commercial Broadcasting	•		

How does it work?

All the versions require the following notice:

```
Copyright (c) <year> by <author's name or designee>.
This material may be distributed only subject to
the terms and conditions set forth in the <fill in
appropriate color> OpenMusic License, vX.Y or later
(the latest version is presently available at http:
//openmusic.linuxtag.org/).
```

The reference must be immediately followed with any options elected by the author(s) and/ or publisher of the work with reference to the medium that they are choosing.

The Green OpenMusic License

Draft v1.1, 22 April 2001

The green music license is based most closely on the GNU GPL and hence grants the widest range of liberties.

Rights granted

A musician making his/ her work available under the Green OpenMusic License grants the licensee the following rights:

1. **Reproduction**: The right to reproduce the work in whole or in part in any medium, physical or electronic provided that the terms of this license are adhered to, and the licensee who is making a repro duction makes it known that the work is licensed under the terms of the Green License.
2. **Commercial redistribution**: The right to redistribute includes commercial redistribution.

How does it work?

Any publication in physical form (like a CD) requires the citation of the original publisher and author. The publisher and author's names must appear on all outer surfaces of the product. On all outer surfaces of the product the original publisher's name shall be as large as the title of the work and cited as possessive with respect to the title.

Specific medium: The musician retains the copyright of the work and grants rights under this license for a specified medium. He or she may choose to license another format under a different license. Thus the terms of the license may be limited only to digital distribution over the internet, in which case the licensee would not have the same rights with respect to cassettes or CD's. Permission can however be obtained from the copyright holder for any other medium. This option is called the Media Locking option.

To accomplish this, add the phrase "`Distribution of the work or derivative of the work is restricted to <insert medium here> unless prior permission is obtained from the copyright holder.`" to the license distributed with the work.

Scope

If the licensee includes an OpenMusic work or a part of a collection with other works, the license does not become automatically applicable to the other works. Thus you could have a CD with ten songs, and two of these are licensed under the terms of OpenMusic. This does not make the other eight subject to the OpenMusic license. However there should be a notice which informs people about the works that are OpenMusic works.

As with most open content licenses, the works are licensed as is and there are no warranties provided.

If the license makes any modifications, the following requirements must be satisfied:

- All modified versions of works are covered by this license. This includes a new work that incorporates a part of an OpenMusic work
- The modified version must be labeled as such.
- The person making the modifications must be identified and the modifications dated.
- The location of the original unmodified work must be identified.

- The original musician's name(s) may not be used to assert or imply endorsement of the resulting work without the original author's (or authors') permission.
- The new work has to be released under precisely this License, with the modified version filling the role of the work, thus licensing distribution and modification of the modified version to whoever possesses a copy of it.

Good-practice recommendations
The license also recommends that if any person is distributing any OpenMusic work in a physical form, they should send a 30 days notification to the original musician/licensor so that it gives him an opportunity to provide an updated work, if s/he has one. The notification should describe any modifications to the work.

It is also suggested that it is considered good form to offer a free copy of any physical form expression of an OpenMusic-licensed work to its author(s).

The Yellow OpenMusic License

Draft v1.1, 22 April 2001

The second in the colorful set of the OpenMusic licenses, the Yellow License is a bit more restrictive than the Green License when it comes to commercial uses. Use this license if you want to allow modifications but the music should be restricted to non-commercial usage. Everything remains the same as the Green License, except that there is one additional clause which restricts any commercial usage without prior permission.

The publication of this work or derivative works in whole or in part in standard (physical) form for commercial purposes is prohibited unless prior permission is obtained from the copyright holder. 'Commercial purposes' include any broadcasting via commercial networks, commercial hiring, commercial copying and lending, and commercial public performance.

The Red OpenMusic License

The most restrictive of all the OpenMusic licenses, this license only allows for three rights.

Rights granted

1. Personal use
2. Personal distribution
3. Personal broadcast

So the rights which are granted in the Green License such as the right to modify, the right to distribute and the right to create derivative works are not allowed under this license. There is also no right to make any commercial usage of the work.

So as you can see, the progression from green to yellow to red is one about a movement from the grant of almost all rights to the grant of very restricted rights.

Creative Commons Licenses

Version 2.0
http://creativecommons.org
http://nl.creativecommons.org

One of the most significant initiatives in the relatively new domain of open content licensing, the Creative Commons have in a short span of time created a buzz around the idea of open content. Backed by solid licenses and highly user-friendly interface, as a way of navigating the site on which their licenses are presented Creative Commons has emerged as the premier destination for people interested in licensing different kinds of content on an open content basis. The web site has a lot of information for a range of users, from the first time user to a list of advanced readings for scholars and researchers. The Creative Commons is also creating a set of international licenses that are customized for different jurisdictions. A Dutch language version is available from the website above, which also provides news and information in Dutch.

Philosophy of Creative Commons
Inspired by the free software movement, the Creative Commons believes that a large vibrant public domain of information and content is a pre-requisite to sustained creativity, and there is a need to proactively enrich this public domain by creating a positive rights discourse. It does this by creating a set of licenses to enable open content and collaboration, as well as acting as a database of open content. Creative Commons also serves to educate the public about issues of copyright, freedom of speech and expression and the public domain.

How does it work?

Creative Commons have a set of licenses which are created through a license wizard. The wizard offers the end user the ability to make their choices on three key concepts. The combination chosen by the end user determines the final license. The three key concepts are:

1. Attribution

Attribution is the right to be identified as the author of the work. By choosing yes, you essentially allow people to use your work provided that they give you credit and acknowledge your authorship. It is to be noted that Creative Commons Ver. 2 makes attribution the default rule since over 95% of the people who used CC licenses had chosen 'yes' to the attribution choice.

2. Commercial Use

This choice basically determine whether you will allow any person to make a commercial use of your work, or if it will only be allowed for non-commercial purposes.

3. Modification/ Creation of Derivative works

The second choice determines the ability for people to create derivative works from your work. By choosing no to this option, you allow people to access, make copies, distribute, display and perform your works verbatim. But they are not allowed to make derivate works based upon it. You may allow yes to this option, without any conditions, in which case people are free to make derivative works without any restrictions. You may also choose yes, but impose a condition that the derivative work will have to be licensed under the same terms and conditions that govern your work. In other words, a person making a derivative work from your work will not be allowed to add any additional restrictions on other people using the work of making derivatives of that work.

In the first version of Creative Commons, you could technically come up with eleven kinds of licenses, based on a combination of attribution/ derivation/ commercial usage. But now in Version 2, as attribution has been made a default rule, there are only six possible combinations that you can arrive at. These are:

a. Commercial/ Derivation
b. Non Commercial/ Derivation
c. Commercial/ Non derivation
d. Non Commercial/ Non Derivation
e. Commercial/ Derivation but Share Alike
f. Non Commercial/ Derivation but share alike

To make it easier for the end user to use, the same license is presented in three forms:

- As a **Commons Deed**: This is a simple one page, plain-language summary of the license, complete with the relevant icons.
- **Legal Code**. The formal license in legal language
- **Digital Code**. A metadata translation of the license that helps search engines and other applications identify the work by its terms of use.

In addition to these basic licenses, Creative Commons also offers a few special licenses such as:

- **Public Domain Dedication**
  This is when you effectively want to relinquish your copyright, and do not want to control any rights at all. It is a 'No Rights Reserved' decision

- **Founder's copyright**
  A method through which you adopt a shorter term for your copyright, namely 14 years, extendable by another fourteen, rather than the seventy years after death of author rule of the US Copyright Act.

- **Mash Me**
  The sampling license that enables people to creatively rework your content in full or in part.

- **Share Music**
  a license that allows people to download, copy, file-share, trade, distribute, and publicly perform your music but does not allow them to make derivative works or make any commercial usage of it. This is the equivalent of a non commercial, non derivation license but written specifically for musicians.

Baseline rights and restrictions in all licenses
All Creative Commons licenses have many important features in common.

Every license:
- Asserts your copyright over the work, and then allows you to determine the manner and extent to which you are willing to grant people freedoms to your work.
- Makes it clear that the license does not affect the fair use rights that a person may have with respect to the work, and that it does not limit in any manner rights that you may acquire on the basis of the 'first sale doctrine' or your freedom of speech and expression.

Note: The 'first sale doctrine' in copyright essentially stipulates that any person who buys a commodity which is also the subject of copyright is free thereafter to transact with that copy (for instance, if I buy a book I am free to sell it to a second hand store).

Every license requires licensees:

- to obtain your permission do any of the things that you may have chosen to restrict. Thus, for example, if you have chosen a license that only allows people to access, copy and distribute your work, then they will have to obtain your permission if they want to make a commercial use of the work or want to create a derivative work.
- to keep any copyright notice intact on all copies of your work, when they distribute the work.
- publish the license with the work or to link to your license from copies of the work.
- not to alter the terms of the license.
- not to use technology or any other means to restrict other licensees' lawful uses of the work.

Every license allows licensees (provided they live up to your conditions) to:

- copy the work
- distribute the work
- display or perform it publicly
- make digital public performances of the work (e.g., webcasting)
- shift the work into another format as a ***verbatim copy***

Every license:

- applies worldwide
- lasts for the duration of the work's copyright
- is ***non-revocable***

The standard terms and conditions apply for all licenses, and the areas of difference between the various licenses, as stated before, really depends on the combination of two primary ingredients, whether you allow commercial use, and whether you allow the creation of derivative works (and, if so, under what conditions).

We can now return to the six basic licenses that can emerge based on your preferences while navigating through the Creative Commons License Wizard.

a. Commercial/ Derivation

This is the broadest license that is available under the CC Package. It grants the end user all the rights including the right to create derivative works, as well as the right to commercially exploit the work. There are also very few restrictions that are imposed by this license, apart from crediting the author where necessary, and following the other procedural requirements, such as maintaining the notices of the license.

This license does not even require the user to distribute his or her derivative works under the terms of the Creative Commons license. S/he is even free to impose ordinary copyright terms which are restrictive on the derivative work.

b. Non-Commercial/ Derivation

Under this license the end user is granted all rights, provided that they do not make any commercial use of the work without your permission. The user however has the right to make derivative work. It is to be noted that for the purpose of this license, file-sharing or other means of sharing the work on a non-monetary basis is not considered a commercial use.

c. Commercial/ Non Derivation

This license is in many ways the reverse of the previous one. Under this license, you are allowed to make commercial use of the work but you are not allowed to make any derivative works based on the original work.

d. Non Commercial/ Non Derivation

This license is perhaps the most restrictive license as it grants the user no rights apart from the baseline rights, namely the right to use, copy, distribute and perform the work. The end user however has no right either to make a derivative work or to make any commercial use of the work.

The last two licenses come closer to the GNU GPL family in that they impose restrictions on the way that the end user may deal with the question of how derivative works are to be dealt with. The term that is used in the last two licenses is 'share alike', which means that the end user is allowed to exercise the right to create a derivative work only if s/he also allows the same rights to others.

e. Commercial/ Derivation but Share Alike

Under this license, the user is granted all rights including the right to make commercial exploitation of the work as well as to create derivative works. The only condition is that the same rights have to be granted by the user with respect to the derivative work that s/he produces. Thus even taking the example from within the Creative Commons licenses, an end user who uses a work based on this license cannot then license his work out under any of the non derivation licenses. In other words s/he cannot then impose any restriction on the right to create derivative works. This license, like the GNU GPL, has a self-perpetuating quality as it travels from person to person ensuring that the original freedoms granted are not curtailed.

f. Non Commercial/ Derivation but Share Alike

Similar to the previous license, the only condition imposed here is that there will be no commercial use of the works.

Other Licenses

Open Content and Open Publication License

http://www.opencontent.org

The Open Content and Open Publication Licenses were drafted by Dr. David Wiley, Assistant Professor of Instructional Technology at Utah State University. It was one of the first attempts to translate the terms of the FLOSS model into the non-software model. These are perhaps only of academic or historical value now, as the open content site has been officially closed since early 2004 and the licenses have been replaced by the Creative Commons licenses. In his words:

> "OpenContent is officially closed. And that's just fine. My main goal in beginning OpenContent back in the Spring of 1998 was to evangelize a way of thinking about sharing materials, especially those that are useful for supporting education. Here is a brief end of project report. In the Spring of 1998 I coined the term "open content" and began evangelizing the idea. As of today, Google knows about over 125,000 uses of the term 'open content' or opencontent. Google and DMOZ both have categories for 'Open Content'. Harvard Law uses the term. We've been mentioned by the New York Times, The Economist, MIT Technology Review, Wired, Reuters, and others popular news media. Creative Commons at Stanford Law has cited OpenContent as a major inspiration. MIT has opened its content with its

> OpenCourseWare initiative, CMU has its Open Learning Initiative, and other schools are following. Several printed books have been published under the OPL. &c. All told, I think we're off to a dandy start. I'm closing OpenContent because I think Creative Commons is doing a better job of providing licensing options which will stand up in court"

It is important to acknowledge Wiley's open mindedness about a development on the open content license. I think it is a great gesture of moving away from an authorial framework to a more collaborative set up. It is however useful for us to understand these two licenses. Firstly, they are and always will be applicable to works that have been published under these licenses. Secondly it is helpful to understand the initial efforts in the move to the open content model.

The Open Content License

Ver 1.0, July 14, 1998

Philosophy of the Open Content license

The license follows the FLOSS model but attempts to include the larger world of content. 'Content' is not defined, which makes the license applicable to any medium. The license was drafted keeping academic needs in mind, making it possible for people to share their work.

Rights Granted

Following in the footsteps of the GNU GPL, the Open Content License also works on the fundamental premise of freedom for the end user. In this case there are three fundamental freedoms that are granted:

1. The right to make copies
2. The right to redistribute the content
3. The right to modify the content

How does it work?

The license allows:

1. The right to make copies

2. The right to redistribute the content

When you license a work under the Open Content License, you grant the licensee the right to copy and distribute exact replicas of the OpenContent (OC) in any medium. The licensee however has to ensure that:

- s/he conspicuously and appropriately publish on each copy an appropriate copyright notice and disclaimer of warranty.
- keep intact all the notices that refer to this License and to the absence of any warranty; (See below) and give any other recipients of the OC a copy of this License along with the OC.

Note on the warranty clause: One of the critical components of the licensing model starting from the GNU GPL is that the licenses are very clear that the product/software comes without any warranties. All open content licenses that have attempted to model themselves on the GNU GPL follow the same pattern, and the 'no warranty' clause is very important. What it basically does is to protect the licensor from any legal claim made by a user of the content, since the licensor is only making the work available as it is, and does not provide any warrant on it. Under the Open Content license, the licensee is allowed to charge a fee for the media (e.g. floppy disk, CD ROM etc.) and/or handling involved in creating a unique copy of the Open Content for use offline.

The licensee may also charge a fee for instructional support for the open content. You may at your discretion offer warranty in exchange for a fee. This is less like a warranty and more like a service charge, since the content itself does not come with any warranty.

The licensee can however not charge a fee for the Open Content itself, or for making it available where there is no tangible medium involved (thus someone sending it via the internet or FTP cannot charge).

3. Right to Modify
The licensee can modify the work. These modifications become 'works based on the Content' and have to be distributed on the same terms and conditions as the Open Content license.

In addition, the license must ensure the following:
- The modified content must carry prominent notices documenting the changes including the exact details, nature and content of the changes, and the date of any change.
- The modified work has to be licensed at no charge to all third parties under the terms of the License.

These conditions do not apply to instances where you can distinguish between works that have been based on Open Content and those that have not. For instance you may have an anthology of poems, where some of the poems were based on Open Content while others are not. In such cases it does not mean that the entire anthology will be subject to the Open Publication License.

Open Publication License
v1.0, 8 June 1999

If you pick up any ordinary book, you will always find in the first few pages a copyright notice that generally says "*All rights reserved. No part of this book may be reproduced, distributed, in full or in part without the permission of the publishers*".

This is a typical publication license which means that you can only use the book/ article by reading it, and you have no right to reproduce it for instance in a compilation that you are bringing out.

The Open Publication License attempts to reverse this by making all publications licensed under it freely available for reproduction, distribution and modification.

Medium it applies to
No longer in use. Was used for any kind of publication including documentation. It must be stated that this license, being an early generattion of open content license is not one of the clearest. Now, for purposes of publication it might be more appropriate to use either a Creative Commons license or for the purposes of documentation, to use the GNU Free Documentation License.

How does it work?
The primary reason for the absence of clarity is a clause in the license (Clause 6) which allows a person to impose certain licensing options, or restrictions, which alters the nature of the license and transforms it from being a free license to a relatively non free license.

Clause 6 of the license basically allows the licensor the ability to add a clause which says that no substantive modifications may be made and distributed without the expression permission of the licensor. It seeks to accomplish the task of two kinds of licenses within the same license. That can be confusing both for the licensor and the user. The Creative Commons have solved this problem by having various combinations, so that if you choose to not allow people to distribute modified versions of your work, then it is under a separate license altogether.

Design Science License

Copyright © 1999-2000
http://www.rare-earth-magnets.com/magnet_university/design_science_license.htm

The Design Science License is a general copyleft license that attempts to accommodate all kind of works, but is particularly suited for media works.

Philosophy of the Design Science License

The preamble of the license begins with a general statement of what copyleft seeks to do, and pitches itself in opposition to the exclusions of copyright. It situates itself clearly within a 'socially relevant' practice of science and arts and states that "`Whereas 'design science' is a strategy for the development of artifacts as a way to reform the environment (not people) and subsequently improve the universal standard of living, this Design Science License was written and deployed as a strategy for promoting the progress of science and art through reform of the environment`".

Medium it applies to

The license is generally applicable to all works that may be protected under copyright, and the definition of "work" also includes any derivative work that may be created from a work licensed under the DSL.

Importantly, the Design Science License also requires that both the 'object form' (the work in a presentation format, like a PDF or an mp3 file) and the 'source data' (the file in which the work was originally authored) are distributed under its terms; plus any accompanying files necessary for the installation, configuration or compilation of the work.

Example: If the work is a text document composed and edited in the LaTeX format, then the original LaTeX file is the source data, and a PDF document generated from it is the object form. If the work is an mp3 audio file exported from an audio sequencer program, then the original sequencer file and all sound samples used are the source data.

Rights Granted

The license grants the user the right to copy, distribute and modify copies of the Work.

How does it work?

1. Right to copy

The license grants the right to distribute and publish verbatim copies of the entire Source Data of the Work, in any medium, if the full copyright notice and disclaimer of warranty is conspicuously published on all copies, and a copy of this License is distributed along with the Work.

With respect to the distribution and publication of the object form of the work, any one of the following conditions have to be met:

- The Source Data should included in the same distribution, distributed under the terms of this License; or
- A written offer is included with the distribution, valid for at least three years or for as long as the distribution is in print, with a publicly-accessible address (such as a URL on the Internet) where, for a charge not greater than transportation and media costs, anyone may receive a copy of the Source Data of the Work
- A third party's written offer for obtaining the Source Data at no cost, is included with the distribution. This option is valid only if is the licensee is a non-commercial party, and only if s/he received the Object Form of the Work along with such an offer.

The licensee may copy and distribute the Work either ***gratis*** or for a fee, and may also offer a warranty protection if desired, you may offer warranty protection for the Work.

2. Right to modify the work

The license allows for a right to modify the work and create to a derivate work provided:

- The new, derivative work is published under the terms of this License.
- The derivative work is given a new name, so that its name or title can not be confused with the Work, or with a version of the Work, in any way.
- Appropriate authorship credit is given: for the differences between the Work and the new derivative work, authorship is attributed to the licensee, while the material sampled or used from the Work remains attributed to the original Author; appropriate notice must be included with the new work indicating the nature and the dates of any modifications of the Work made.

No restrictions
The license does not allow the licensee to impose any further restrictions on the Work or any of its derivative works beyond those restrictions described in the License.

Ethymonics Free Music License

Version 1, August 2000
http://www.ethymonics.co.uk/fmlinfo.html

Ethymonics is a small music company that sells free music. Reversing the general presumption that downloading free music hurts the music industry, the Ethymoncs license is designed to use free music as a way of promoting artists.

According to them "`By permitting others to make copies of the music, and even to sell those copies, the music becomes widely known. If you like the music, then you can buy the artist's CD or go to see them play live. Ethymonics is a company that sells Free Music. We pay` `the artist a royalty, so people can buy a CD from us to support the artist, as well as get a high quality CD"`

Philosophy
The preamble to the license reiterates the principles of the GNU GPL and the free software movement, that the word 'free' refers to freedom and not to price. Hence it is a license that is modeled on the principle of the GNU GPL. See http://www.ethymonics.co.uk/philos.html for a text outlining their philosophy.

Medium it applies to
The license is applicable for musical works, and this includes the work, whether in a recording, performance or other form of musical representation, or any derivative work.

Rights Granted
The license grants the licensee the following rights:

1. Right to access the musical work

2. Right to make copies and distribute the musical work
Provided the licensee fulfills the following requirements:

- conspicuously and appropriately publish on each copy an appropriate copyright notice;
- keep intact all the notices that refer to this License;
- supply, with each copy of the Music, all significant information about the Music, including the title of the work, the name of the artist, and the names and roles of all credited personnel;
- supply, to each recipient of the Music, along with the Music, either a copy of this License or a website where it is available

In case any part of the above information is not available, for example when the Music has been received by making a recording of a performance, then this information must be obtained independently and no copies can be made or distributed without this information being included with each copy of the Music.

3. The right to play or perform the Music publicly
For example in a broadcast, provided that you make available to listeners the title of the work and the name of the Artist. In case a recording is made of such performance, then it also falls under the provision of this license

4. A recording made as a result of the music being played or performed is covered by this License when its contents constitute a work based on the music. The license must be made available to listeners.

5. The right to make copies of such a recording
Provided that the license is also made available.

No restrictions
The license does not allow the licensee either to sub-license or impose any restrictions on the work or any derivative works.

additional readings

Open Source/ Free Software

Yochai Benkler, *Coase's Penguin, or, Linux and the Nature of the Firm*, Yale L. Jour, December 2002, 369

Magnus Bergquist and Jan Ljungberg. *The Power of Gifts: Organising Social Relationships in Open Source Communities*. Information Systems Journal, 11(4):305-320, 2001.

Nikolai Bezroukov. *A Second Look at the Cathedral and Bazaar*. First Monday, 4(12), December 1999.

E. Gabriella Coleman and Benjamin Hill. *The Social Production of Ethics in Debian and Free Software Communities: Anthropological Lessons for Vocational Ethic*. In Stefan Koch, editor, *Free/Open Source Software Development*, pages 273-295. Idea Group Publishing, Hershey, PA, 2004.

Chris DiBona, Sam Ockman, and Mark Stone, editors, *Open Sources: Voices from the Open Source Revolution*. O'Reilly and Associates, Cambridge, Massachusetts, 1999.

Joseph Feller and Brian Fitzgerald. *Understanding Open Source Software Development*. Addison-Wesley, London, 2002.

Robert W. Hahn (editor). *Government Policy toward Open Source Software*. AEI-Brookings Joint Center for Regulatory Studies, 2002.

Rishab Aiyer Ghosh and Vipul Ved Prakash. *The Orbiten Free Software Survey*. First Monday, 5(7), July 2000.

Rishab Aiyer Ghosh. *Cooking Pot Markets: an Economic Model for the Trade in Free Goods and Services on the Internet*. First Monday, 3(3), March 1998.

Andrius Kulkikauskas and David Ellison Bey, *An Economy of Giving Everything Away*, **http://www.ms.lt/en/workingopenly/givingaway.html**

Brian Martin, *Against Intellectual Property*, **http://danny.oz.au/free-software/advocacy/against_IP.html**

Eben Moglen. *Anarchism Triumphant: Free Software and the Death of Copyright*. First Monday, 4(8), August 1999.

John Kelsey and Bruce Schneier. *The Street Performer Protocol and Digital Copyrights*. First Monday, 4(6), June 1999.

Sandeep Krishnamurthy. *Cave or Community? an Empirical Investigation of 100 Mature Open Source Projects*. First Monday, 7(6), June 2002.

David Lancashire. *Code, Culture and Cash: The Fading Altruism of Open Source Development*. First Monday, 6(12), December 2001.

Lawrence Lessig, *Commons and Code*, 1999 Fordham Intellectual Property, Media and Entertainment Law

Wu Ming, *Call It As You Like, It's Freedom, and That's What Counts*, **http://www.wumingfoundation.com/italiano/outtakes/note_on_copyleft.html**

Jan Newmarch. *Lessons from Open Source: Intellectual Property and Courseware*. First Monday, 6(6), June 2001.

Niranjan Ranjani, *Free as in Education*, **http://www.itu.int/wsis/docs/background/themes/access/free_as_in_education_niranjan.pdf**

Eric S. Raymond. *A Brief History of Hackerdom*. In Chris DiBona, Sam Ockman, and Mark Stone, editors, *Open Sources: Voices from the Open Source Revolution*. O'Reilly and Associates, Cambridge, Massachusetts, 1999.

Eric S. Raymond. *The Cathedral and the Bazaar: Musings on Linux and Open Source by an Accidental Revolutionary*. O'Reilly and Associates, Sebastopol, California, 1999.

John Söderberg. *Copyleft vs. Copyright: A Marxist Critique*. First Monday, 7(3), March 2002.

Richard M. Stallman. *Free Software, Free Society: Selected Essays of Richard M. Stallman*. GNU Press, Boston, Massachusetts, 2002.

Richard M. Stallman. *The GNU Operating System and the Free Software Movement*. In Chris DiBona, Sam Ockman, and Mark Stone, editors, *Open Sources: Voices from the Open Source Revolution*. O'Reilly and Associates, Cambridge, Massachusetts, 1999.

Robert Young. *Giving it Away: How Red Hat Software Stumbled Across a New Economic Model and Helped Improve an Industry*. In Chris DiBona, Sam Ockman, and Mark Stone, editors, *Open Sources: Voices from the Open Source Revolution*. O'Reilly and Associates, Cambridge, Massachusetts, 1999.

David Zeitlyn. *Gift Economies in the Development of Open Source Software: Anthropological Reflections*. Research Policy, 32(7):1287-1291, 2003.

Cultural Production/ Copyright and Culture

Yochai Benkler, *An Unhurried View Of Private Ordering in Information Transactions*, Vanderbilt Law Review 2063

Yochai Benkler, *Free as the Air to Common Use: First Amendment Constraints on Enclosure of the Public*

Domain, New York University Law Review, May, 1999, 354

Josephine Berry, *Bare Code: Net Art and the Free Software Movement*, **http://netartcommons.walkerart.org/article.pl?sid=02/05/08/0615215&mode=thread**

Margaret Chon, *New Wine Bursting from Old Bottles: Collaborative Internet Art, Joint Works, And Entrepreneurship*, Oregon Law Review, Spring 1996, 297

Biella Coleman, *The Social Creation of Productive Freedom: Free Software Hacking and the Redefinition of Labor, Authorship, and Creativity*, **http://www.healthhacker.com/biella/proposal2.html**

Rochelle Cooper Dreyfuss, *Collaborative Research: Conflicts on Authorship, Ownership, and Accountability*, 53 Vand. L. Rev. 1162

Brian Drobnik, *How the Grateful Dead Turned Alternative Business and Legal Strategies Into A Great American Success Story*, 2 Vand. J. Ent. L. & Prac. 242

Christopher D. Hunter, *Copyright and Culture*, **http://www.asc.upenn.edu/usr/chunter/**

Rishab Aiyar Ghosh, *Free Software and the Death of Copyright*, available at **http://www.firstmonday.org**

Jon Ippolito, *Why Art Should Be Free*, **http://www.culturekitchen.com/archives/000482.html**

Lawrence Lessig, *Free Culture.* Pengiun, London, 2004 available at **http://www.lessig.org**

Cesar Nunes, *Collaborative Content Creation by Cross Level Students*, **http://www.thinkcycle.org/tc-filesystem/file?file_id=37480**

Nitin Sawhney, *Cooperative Innovation in the Commons*, **http://web.media.mit.edu/~nitin/thesis/**

Peter Shand, *Scenes from the Colonial Catwalk: Cultural Appropiation, Intellectual Property Rights and Fashion*,

http://ist-socrates.berkeley.edu/~caforum/volume3/pdf/shand.pdf

Ruth Towse, *Copyright Policy and Creativity in the Cultural Industries*, **http://cost-a20.iscte.pt/tromso/Copyright_Policy_and_Creativity.doc**

Reuben Van Wendel de Joode et al, *Protecting the Virtual Commons,* **http://www.webster-dictionary.org/definition/Protecting%20the%20Virtual%20Commons**

Legal Aspects of Open Source/ Open Content Licensing

Severine Dusollier, *Open Source and Copyleft: Authorship Reconsidered*? Columbia Journal of Law & the Arts, Summer 2003, 281

Vincent van den Eijnde, *Auteursrecht voor Ontwerpers*, BNO, Amsterdam, 2003

Robert W. Gomulkiewicz, *How Copyleft Uses License Rights To Succeed in the Open Source Software Revolution and the Implications for Article 2b*

Robert W. Gomulkiewicz, *De-Bugging Open Source Software Licensing*, Univ. of Pittsburg Law. Rev, 75

David McGowan, *Legal Implications of Open Source Software*, http://papers.ssrn.com/sol3/papers.cfm?abstract_id=243237 *Houston law Rev.*, Spring 1999

Ira V Heffan, *Copyleft: Licensing Collaborative Works in the Digital Age*, 49 Stan. L. Rev. 1487

Teresa Hill, *Fragmenting the Copyleft Movement: The Public Will Not Prevail*, 1999 Utah L. Rev. 797

Natsha Horne, *Open Source Software Licensing: Using Copyright Law to Encourage Free Use*, 17 Ga. St. U.L. Rev. 863

Jeffrey Lee, *Open Source Software Licenses and Innovation*, **http://VirtualGoods.tu-ilmenau.de/2003/licenses_innovation_leejz.pdf**

Stephen Mcjohn, *The Paradoxes of Free Software*, 9 Geo. Mason L. Rev. 25

Christian Nadan, *Open Source Licensing: Virus or Virtue? Texas Intellectual Property Law Journal*, Spring 2002, 349

Shawn Potter, *Opening Up to Open Source*, 6 Rich. J.L. & Tech. 24

Josh Terner and Jean Tirole, *Scope of Open Source Licensing*, **http://papers.ssrn.com/sol3/papers.cfm?abstract_id=359303**

Jason Wacha, *Open Source, Free Software, and the General Public License, Computer and Internet Lawyer*, March 2003, 20

glossary

Attribution

Attribution means simply that the author of a piece of work of whatever kind is credited with their part in the work in an accompanying text, strapline, colophon in the case or an image or sound recording or in the case of a text, in an appropriate place according to the conventions of the specific media.

Author

The author of a work is the person, company or other entity which is deemed to have produced it. The author of a book is the person who wrote it. The author of a website might be one or several people.

Cease and desist letter

A letter from a lawyer requested or insisting that what they understand to be a copyright infringement stop.

Commons

The commons are resources or goods held in common, that are owned by all and could not or should not be turned into property or diminished. Air is a good example of a commons.

Copyleft

Copyleft is phrase first used by artist Ray Johnson to describe the way he mixed images together from various media sources and then made them available by ephemeral means such as mail art or as gifts. The phrase has since been used by Free Software developers to name their variant use of copyright law.

Copyright
A set of laws, originally designed to protect publishing monopolies, which give those who purchase or otherwise obtain a license from authors to have rights over their work's publication.

Creator
(see Author)

Derivative Work
A derivative work is something that uses as an element in its composition a part or even the whole of another work. Sample-based music is often derivative for instance. The theory of derivation requires that there be a fixed and unmoving point of origination. A theory of culture which sees it as a matter of flows, change and emergent collaboration would claim that all work is derivative.

FLOSS
'Free/Libre and Open Source Software' (see page 24)

Fair Use
Fair use rights are those which allow you, if you are for instance writing an academic paper or a review of a book or website to quote that material.

GNU GPL
The GNU GPL (online at **http://www.fsf.org/copyleft/gpl/html**) is a license for software which guarantees

continuing rights to these freedoms: "*The freedom to run the program, for any purpose (freedom 0).The freedom to study how the program works, and adapt it to your needs (freedom 1). Access to the source code is a precondition for this. The freedom to redistribute copies so you can help your neighbor (freedom 2). Freedom to improve the program, and release your improvements to the public, so that the whole community benefits (freedom 3). Access to the source code is a precondition for this.*" This definition of freedom is taken from the Free Software Foundation website:
http://wwww.fsf.org/

Gratis
Without any financial cost.

Infringement
In the case of copyright, an infringement is usually using copyrighted material without receiving permission from the author or owner of the copyright.

Liability
To have a responsibility for or to be subject to the consequences of something.

License
A document which sets the terms of use of a piece of software or other item of culture. A user is licensed to use the material in certain ways. This booklet lists licenses which set out to maximize the usefulness of such material.

Open Content
Here this is used as a generic term. Content is any material, data, files, images, texts, which are not part of software

or other digital systems but which are handled by them. 'Open' content is any such content which is made available by means of one of the kinds of licenses described in this booklet. One of the licenses described here, 'Open Content' (see page 86) which has now been subsumed by the Creative Commons project also used this term.

Peer to peer (P2P)
A system by which files can be shared over a network, often the internet. Usually peer to peer systems are arranged in a distributed network which makes users simultaneously a hub and a node. P2P systems to look for are, amongst others, BitTorrent, GNUtella and Kazaa.

Preamble
The opening statements to a license that do not usually form part of its legally applicable terms. The preamble is important to understand legal documents also as a form of narrative in which certain ideas and norms are invented and circulated.

Proprietary
Something that is owned by a company and which is so formatted that it does not allow access to its source code.

Public Domain
Something in the public domain is available for anyone to use regardless of copyright.

(Non)Revocable
A license is revocable if you can change its terms after something has been made public. Usually licenses are non-revocable.

Royalties
A proportion of the profit assigned to an author after publishers, distributors and other have taken their (usually larger) percentages.

Source Code
Source code is what a programmer works on in a programming language before it is compiled (turned into machine code). For FLOSS it is essential therefore that the source code be accessible to allow others to work on and improve it.

Verbatim Copy
A full and complete copy without any changes.

Warranty
A warranty is usually a guarantee that things are of a certain quality, that they will not fail to work under normal circumstances of use. Software for instance is usually issued without a warranty.

Colophon

About the author

Lawrence Liang is a legal researcher with the Alternative Law Forum (ALF) in Bangalore. His key areas of interest are law, technology and culture, the politics of copyright and he has been working closely with Sarai, New Delhi on a joint research project *Intellectual Property and the Knowledge/ Culture Commons*. A keen follower of the open source movement in software, Lawrence has been working on ways of translating the open source ideas into the cultural domain. He has written a number of articles on copyright, free software and media practices, and in collaboration with Sarai also wrote the license for OPUS, an online collaborative platform for artists and media practitioners. In 2004 he was a Research Fellow at Media Design Research, Piet Zwart Institute, Rotterdam.

Alternative Law Forum: **http://www.altlawforum.org/**
Sarai: **http://www.sarai.net/**
OPUS: **http://www.opuscommons.net/**

Additional material, chapter 1: Florian Cramer
Editors: Florian Cramer, Matthew Fuller, Calum Selkirk
Graphic design: Femke Snelting
Printed by: De Maasstad, Rotterdam

December 2004
Media Design Research, Piet Zwart Institute,
Willem de Kooning Academy Hogeschool Rotterdam
http://www.pzwart.wdka.hro.nl